Welcome to Country

T0362819

We Welcome You

Welcome to Country is **special**.

Welcome to Country is a way to say come in, we welcome you.

Here is the music at Welcome to Country.

This is the dance at Welcome to Country.

7

This is the **smoke** at Welcome to Country.

When we are at school, we will have a Welcome to Country.

When we are at the game, we will have a Welcome to Country.

When we are here,
we will have a
Welcome to Country.

When we are here,
we will have a
Welcome to Country.

Welcome to Country is special for us.

Glossary

smoke

special